William Miller

Scottish Nursery Songs, and Other Poems

William Miller

Scottish Nursery Songs, and Other Poems

ISBN/EAN: 9783337240936

Printed in Europe, USA, Canada, Australia, Japan

Cover: Foto ©Thomas Meinert / pixelio.de

More available books at **www.hansebooks.com**

SCOTTISH

Nursery Songs,

And other Poems.

BY WILLIAM MILLER.

" Breathe in their ear those russet hymns,
Whose music floods and overbrims
  The human hearts of all;
For, it is all a mother's art
To win the *spirit* by the *heart*."

GLASGOW:
KERR & RICHARDSON, 89 QUEEN STREET.
1863.

TO SCOTTISH MOTHERS,

GENTLE AND SEMPLE,

These Nursery Songs are respectfully Dedicated,

NOT FEARING THAT, WHILE IN SUCH KEEPING,

THEY WILL EVER BE FORGOT.

WILLIAM MILLER.

Contents.

Address to Mr. William Miller,

AUTHOR OF "WEE WILLIE WINKIE," &c.

Thae bonny sangs ye sing, Willie,
  Wi' sic a touching art,
Round a' our feelings seem to cling,
  An' thrill the very heart.

A mither's love ye've seen, Willie;
  A faither's joy ye've felt;
Or else thae simple strains, I ween,
  Our feelings wadna melt.

The sweet and gladsome lay that's sung,
  Wi' sic a fervent power,
Is like the hinny blab that's wrung
  Frae out the modest flower.

There's magic in that simple lay—
  Sic music in its strain,
That thoughts, receding, bring the ray
  O' bairn-time back again.

We feel the freshness o' the spring,
    In Willie Winkie's glee:
Or whan we hear a mither sing
    Your "Gree, bairns, gree."

The bees that 'mang the blossoms flit
    Wi' laden limbs, may rove;
The mellow fruit is only fit
    To tempt the hornet's love.

Then paint me nature's burstin' bud—
    Man in his artless time,
Ere vice's taint has flush'd his blood,
    Or stained his form wi' crime.

And raise frae virtue's simple style,
    A halo round thy name
That ithers tyne, wha fight and toil
    To gain a brighter fame.

15th October, 1842.   By the late WM. AIR FOSTER.

NURSERY SONGS,

AND OTHER POEMS.

Willie Winkie.

AIR BY REV. WILLIAM BECKETT.

Wee Willie Winkie
    Rins through the toun,
Up stairs and doun stairs
    In his nicht-gown,
Tirling at the window,
    Crying at the lock,
" Are the weans in their bed,
    For it's now ten o'clock?

" Hey, Willie Winkie,
    Are ye coming ben?
The cat's singing grey thrums
    To the sleeping hen,

The dog's spelder'd on the floor,
And disna gie a cheep,
But here's a waukrife laddie
That winna fa' asleep."

Onything but sleep, you rogue!
Glow'ring like the moon,
Rattling in an airn jug
Wi' an airn spoon,
Rumblin', tumblin', round about,
Crawing like a cock,
Skirlin' like a kenna-what,
Wauk'nin' sleeping folk.

"Hey, Willie Winkie—
The wean's in a creel!
Wamblin' aff a body's knee
Like a very eel,
Ruggin' at the cat's lug,
Rav'llin' a' her thrums—
Hey, Willie Winkie—
See, there he comes!"

Wearied is the mither
That has a stoorie wean,
A wee stumpie stousie,
That canna rin his lane.

That has a battle aye wi' sleep,
  Before he'll close an e'e—
But a kiss frae aff his rosy lips
  Gies strength anew to me.

Gree, Bairnies, Gree.

AIR—"Oh, no, we never mention her."

The moon has rowed her in a cloud,
  Stravaging win's begin
To shuggle and daud the window-brods,
  Like loons that wad be in!
Gae whistle a tune in the lum-head,
  Or craik in saughen tree!
We're thankfu' for a cozie hame—
  Sae gree, my bairnies, gree.

Though gurgling blasts may dourly blaw,
  A rousing fire will thow
A straggler's taes, and keep fu' cosh
  My tousie taps-o'-tow.

O who would cule your kail, my bairns,
Or bake your bread like me?
Ye'd get the bit frae out my mouth,
Sae gree, my bairnies, gree.

Oh, never fling the warmsome boon
O' bairnhood's love awa';
Mind how ye sleepit, cheek to cheek,
Between me and the wa';
How ae kind arm was owre ye baith:
But, if ye disagree,
Think on the saft and kindly soun'
O' "Gree, my bairnies, gree."

The Sleepy Laddie.

Are ye no gaun to wauken th' day, ye rogue?
Your parritch is ready and cool in the cog,
Auld baudrons sae gaucy, and Tam o' that ilk
Would fain ha'e a drap o' my wee laddie's milk.

There's a wee birdie singing, get up, get up !
And listen, it says " tak' a whup, tak a whup ;"
But I'll kittle his bosie—a far better plan—
Or pouther his pow wi' a watering can.

There's claes to wash, and the house to redd,
And I canna begin till I mak' the bed ;
For I count it nae brag to be clever as some,
Wha while thrang at a' bakin', can soop the lum.

It's far i' the day now, and brawly ye ken,
Your faither has scarcely a minute to spen' ;
But ae blink o' his wife wi' the bairn on her knee,
He says lightens his toil, tho' sair it may be.

So up to your parritch, and on wi' your claes ;
There's a fire that might warm the cauld Norlan braes ;
For a coggie weel fill'd and a clean fire-en'
Should mak' ye jump up, and gae skelping ben.

The Wonderfu' Wean.

AIR—"The Campbells are Coming."

Our wean's the most wonderfu' wean e'er I saw,
It would tak' me a lang summer day to tell a'
His pranks, frae the morning till night shuts his e'e,
When he sleeps like a peerie, 'tween father and me.
For in his quiet turns, siccan questions he'll speir :
How the moon can stick up in the sky that's sae clear ?
What gars the wind blaw ? and wharfrae comes the rain ?
He's a perfect divert : he's a wonderfn' wean!

Or wha was the first body's father ? and wha
Made the very first snaw-shower that ever did fa' ?
And wha made the first bird that sang on a tree ?
And the water that sooms a' the ships on the sea ?—
But after I've tell't him as weel as I ken,
Again he begins wi' his " Wha ? " and his " When?"
And he looks aye sae watchfu' the while I explain,—
He's as auld as rhe hills—he's an auld-farrant wean.

And folk wha ha'e skill o' the lumps on the head,
Hint there's mae ways than toiling o' winning ane's bread;

How he'll be a rich man, and ha'e men to work for him,
Wi' a kyte like a bailie's, shug-shugging afore him,
Wi' a face like the moon, sober, sonsy, and douce,
And a back, for its breadth, like the side o' a house.
'Tweel I'm unco ta'en up wi't, they mak' a' sae plain ;—
He's just a town's talk—he's a by-ord'nar wean !

I ne'er can forget sic a laugh as I gat,
When I saw him put on father's waistcoat and hat;
Then the lang-leggit boots gaed sae far owre his knees,
The tap loops wi' his fingers he grippit wi' ease,   [ben,
Then he march'd thro' the house, he march'd but, he march'd
Sae like mony mae o' our great little men,
That I leugh clean outright, for I conldna contain,
He was sic a conceit—sic an ancient like wean.

But 'mid a' his daffin' sic kindness he shows,
That he's dear to my heart as the dew to the rose ;
And the unclouded hinnie-beam aye in his e'e,
Mak's him every day dearer and dearer to me.
Though fortune be saucy, and dorty, and dour,
And glooms through her fingers, like hills through a shower,
When bodies hae got ae bit bairn o' their ain,
How he cheers up their hearts,—he's the wonderfu' wean.

Our ain fire-end.

AIR—" Kelvin Grove."

When the frost is on the grun',
  Keep your ain fire-end,
For the warmth o' summer's sun
  Has our ain fire-end;
When there's dubs ye might be lair'd in,
Or snaw wreaths ye could be smoor'd in,
The best flower in the garden
  Is our ain fire-end.

You and father are sic twa!
  Roun' our ain fire-end,
He mak's rabbits on the wa',
  At our ain fire-end.
Then sic fun as they are mumping,
When, to touch them ye gae stumping,
They're set on your tap a-jumping,
  At our ain fire-end.

Sic a bustle as ye keep
  At our ain fire-end,

When ye on your whistle wheep,
　　Round our ain fire-end;
Now, the dog maun get a saddle,
Then a cart's made o' the ladle,
To please ye as ye daidle
　　Round our ain fire-end.

When your head's lain on my lap,
　　At our ain fire-end,
Taking childhood's dreamless nap,
　　At our ain fire-end;
Then frae lug to lug I kiss ye,
An' wi' heart o'erflowing bless ye,
And a' that's gude I wish ye,
　　At our ain fire-end.

When ye're far, far frae the blink
　　O' our ain fire-end,
Fu' monie a time ye'll think
　　On our ain fire-end ;
On a' your gamesome ploys,
On your whistle and your toys,
And ye'll think ye hear the noise
　　O' our ain fire-end.

Cockie-leerie-la.

AIR—"John Anderson, my Jo."

There is a country gentleman,
　Who leads a thrifty life,
Ilk morning scraping orra things
　Thegither for his wife—
His coat o' glowing ruddy brown,
　And wavelet wi' gold—
A crimson crown upon his head,
　Well-fitting one so bold.

If ithers pick where he did scrape,
　He brings them to disgrace,
For, like a man o' metal, he
　Siclike meets face to face;
He gies the loons a lethering,
　A crackit croon to claw—
There is nae gaun about the bush
　Wi Cockie-leerie-la!

His step is firm and evenly,
　His look both sage and grave—

His bearing bold, as if he said,
   "I'll never be a slave!"
And tho' he hauds his head fu' high,
   He glinteth to the grun,
Nor fyles his silver spurs in dubs
   Wi' glowerin' at the sun:

And whiles I've thocht had he a hand
   Wharwi' to grip a stickie,
A pair o' specks across nis neb,
   And round his neck a dickie,
That weans wad laughing haud their sides,
   And cry, " Preserve us a' !
Ye're some frien' to Doctor Drawbluid,
   Douce Cockie-leerie-la !"

So learn frae him to think nae shame
   To work for what ye need,
For he that gapes till he be fed,
   May gape till he be dead;
And if ye live in idleness,
   Ye'll find unto your cost,
That they wha winna work in heat,
   Maun hunger in the frost.

And hain wi' care ilk sair-won plack,
   And honest pride will fill

Your purse wi' gear—ee'n far-off frien's
Will bring grist to your mill;
And if, when grown to be a man,
Your name's without a flaw,
Then rax your neck, and tune your pipes
To Cockie-leerie-la !

Spring.

The Spring comes linking and jinking through the woods,
Opening wi' gentle hand the bonnie green and yellow buds—
There's flowers and showers, and sweet sang o' little bird,
And the gowan wi' his red croon peeping thro' the yird.

The hail comes rattling and brattling snell an' keen,
Dauding and blauding, though red set the sun at e'en ;
In bonnet and wee loof the weans kep and look for mair,
Dancing thro'ther wi' the white pearls shining in their hair.

We meet wi' blythesome an' kythesome cheerie weans,
Daffing and laughing far a-doon the leafy lanes,
Wi' gowans and buttercups busking the thorny wands,
Sweetly singing wi' the flower branch waving in their hands.

'Boon a' that's in thee, to win me, sunny Spring!
Bricht cluds and green buds, and sangs that the birdies sing;
Flower-dappled hill-side and dewy beech sae fresh at e'en;
Or the tappie-toorie fir-tree shining a' in green —

Bairnies, bring treasure and pleasure mair to me,
Stealing and speiling up to fondle on my knee!
In spring-time the young things are blooming sae fresh and fair,
That I canna, Spring, but love and bless thee evermair.

Lady Summer.

AIR—"Blythe, blythe, and merry are we."

Birdie, birdie, weet your whistle!
　　Sing a sang to please the wean;
Let it be o' Lady Summer
　　Walking wi' her gallant train!
Sing him how her gaucy mantle,
　　Forest green trails ower the lea,
Broider'd frae the dewy hem o't
　　Wi' the field flowers to the knee!

How her foot's wi' daisies buskit,
  Kirtle o' the primrose hue,
And her e'e sae like my laddie's,
  Glancing, laughing, loving blue !
How we meet on hill and valley,
  Children sweet as fairest flowers,
Buds and blossoms o' affection,
  Rosy wi' the sunny hours.

Sing him sic a sang, sweet birdie !
  Sing it ower and ower again;
Gar the notes fa' pitter patter,
  Like a shower o' summer rain.
"Hoot, toot, toot!" the birdie's saying,
  "Wha can shear the rigg that's shorn ?
Ye've sung brawlie simmer's ferlies,
  I'll toot on anither horn."

Hairst.

Tho' weel I lo'e the budding spring,
  I'll no misca' John Frost,   •
Nor will I roose the summer days
  At gowden autum's cost ;

For a' the seasons in their turn
　　Some wished-for pleasures bring,
And hand in hand they jink aboot,
　　Like weans at jingo-ring.

Fu' weel I mind how aft ye said,
　　When winter nights were lang,
" I weary for the summer woods,
　　The lintie's tittering sang;
But when the woods grew gay and green,
　　And birds sang sweet and clear,
It then was, " When will hairst-time come,
　　The gloaming o' the year ?"

Oh ! hairst time's like a lipping cup
　　That's gi'en wi' furthy glee !
The fields are fu' o' yellow corn,
　　Red apples bend the tree ;
The genty air, sae ladylike!
　　Has on a scented gown,
And wi' an airy string she leads
　　The thistle-seed balloon.

The yellow corn will porridge mak',
　　The apples taste your mou',

And ower the stibble riggs I'll chase
  The thistle-down wi' you ;
I'll pu' the haw frae aff the thorn,
  The red hip frae the brier——
For wealth hangs in each tangled nook
  In the gloaming o' the year.

Sweet Hope ! ye biggit ha'e a nest
  Within my bairnie's breast—
Oh may his trusting heart ne'er trow
  That whiles ye sing in jest ;
Some coming joys are dancing aye
  Before his langing een,—
He sees the flower that isna blawn,
  And birds that ne'er were seen ;—

The stibble rigg is aye ahin' !
  The gowden grain afore,
And apples drop into his lap,
  Or row in at the door !
Come, hairst-time, then, unto my bairn,
  Drest in your gayest gear,
Wi' saft and winnowing win's to cool
  The gloaming o' the year !

Ye maun Gang to the Schule.

AIR—"As Jenny sat down wi' her wheel by the fire."

Ye maun gang to the schule again' summer, my bairn,
It's no near sae ill as ye're thinking to learn ;
For learning's a' worldly riches aboon—
It's easy to carry, and never gaes done.

Ye'll read o' the land, and ye'll read o' the sea !
O' the high and the low, o' the bound and the free—
And maybe a tear will the wee bookie stain,
When ye read o' the widow and fatherless wean.

And when 'tis a story of storms on the sea,
Where sailors are lost, who have bairnies like thee,
And your heart, growing grit for the fatherless wean,
Gars the tearies hap, hap o'er your cheekies like rain ;

I'll then think on the dew that comes frae aboon,
Like draps frae the stars or the silvery moon,
To freshen the flowers :—but the tears frae your e'e
For the woes ot anither, are dearer to me.

So ye'll gae to the schule again' summer, my bairn—
Ye're sae gleg o' the uptak' ye soon will learn ;—
And I'm sure ere the dark nights o' winter keek ben,
Ye'll can read William Wallace frae en' to en'.

John Frost.

AIR—" The Campbells are coming."

You've come early to see us this year, John Frost,
Wi' your crispin' an' poutherin' gear, John Frost,
    For hedge, tower, an' tree,
    As far as I see,
Are as white as the bloom o' the pear, John Frost

You're very preceese wi' your wark, John Frost !
Altho' ye ha'e wrought in the dark, John Frost,
    For ilka fit-stap,
    Frae the door to the slap,
Is braw as a new linen sark, John Frost.

There are some things about ye I like, John Frost,
And ithers that aft gar me fyke, John Frost;
    For the weans, wi' cauld taes,
    Crying " shoon, stockings, claes,"
Keep us busy as bees in the byke, John Frost.

And gae 'wa' wi' your lang slides, I beg, John Frost!
Bairn's banes are as bruckle's an egg, John Frost;
    For a cloit o' a fa'
    Gars them hirple awa',
Like a hen wi' a happity leg, John Frost.

Ye ha'e fine goings on in the north, John Frost!
Wi' your houses o' ice and so forth, John Frost!
    Tho' their kirn's on the fire,
    They may kirn till they tire,
Yet their butter—pray what is it worth, John Frost?

Now, your breath would be greatly improven, John Frost,
By a scone pipin'-het frae the oven, John Frost;
    And your blae frosty nose
    Nae beauty wad lose,
Kent ye mair baith o' boiling and stovin', John Frost.

The Queen o' Bonny Scotland's a Mither like Mysel'.

There's walth o' themes in Scotland,
  That ham'art tongue might sing
Wi' glee sae canty, that wad mak'
  Its laneliest valleys ring;
But there is ane I dearly lo'e
  In wimplin' sang to swell—
The Queen o' bonny Scotland's
  A mither like mysel'.

Her wee bit rum'lin' roguie,   .
  When rowin' on her knee,
Or cuddlin' in her bosie,
  Will gladden heart an' e'e,
Wi' kissin' owre an' owre again,
  His rosy cheeks will tell—
The Queen o' bonny Scotland's
  A mither like mysel'.

She kens fu' weel how tenderly
    A mither dauts her wean,
And a' the hinnied words that fa'
    Atween them when alane.
Oh ! if I were but near her,
    O' breadless bairns to tell,
She'd listen, for our bonny Queen's
    A mither like mysel'.

Then come to bonny Scotland,
    There's no a neuk in't a',
Frae hill to haugh, that disna bear
    Baith buirdly men and braw;
They'll welcome you to Scotland—
    The thistle and blue-bell—
And ye'se be blessed by women-fock,
    And mithers like yoursel'.

Irish Love Song.

To sing of human happiness, when all is peace and piping,
Or laugh at love and handkerchiefs, when eyelids need no wiping,
Is but to mock the cruel pangs that now my heart is tearing,
And smuder up the hearty groans that's rowling for a hearing:
Och! if I had my paice of mind, that cruel piece of plunder,
I'd let the jades die wrinkled maids, and then they'd see their blunder.

The lovely craturs every one are jewels of perfection,
And mighty need they have, indeed, of comfort and protection;
But I, who'd be their guardian through each future generation;
Am treated like the blackguard scamps that roam about the nation.
Oh paice, throughout the wholesome day, and I, have long been strangers,
And all the night, in woful plight, I dream of fearful dangers.

Where'er I turn my aching eyes for paice or consolation,
Some cheek, or eye, or lip, or brow, works further tribulation—
Och, murther but it seems my fate, that some one will tormint me—
Whene'er I turn me round from one, another is fornint me;
The saucy flirts, if but a word I'd speak of adoration,
With 'Sur!' as sharp's a sword, they'd cut the thread of conversation.

No wonder that the married wives are happy and contented,
Sure of her vows no decent spouse has ever yet repented ;
Whate'er they want their husbands grant, that's fitting for their station,
While nought they do, 'tween me and you, but raising botheration.
Then let the female sex now learn to know what now they're needing,
Nor screw their pretty mouths to No, when Yes would show their breeding.

The Homes and Hearts behind us.

Music by Jesse Williams, Esq.

DEDICATED TO THE SCOTTISH VOLUNTEERS.

Who would not fight for such a land ?—
    The land our fathers bled on
For liberty, with men as bold
    As ever Wallace led on.
Though dear enough our mountain land,
    In serried ranks to bind us
Against all foes ;—yet dearer still
    The homes and hearts behind us.

. Though dear enough our mountain land,
In serried ranks to bind us
Against all foes ;—yet dearer still
The homes and hearts behind us.

Say not that men of other climes
Have stronger arms, or braver,
Or that the land that Freemen own
Hired hordes can e'er enslave her.
Should e'er they touch our dear lov'd shores,
A wall of steel they'll find us ;
For Gallic sword shall never reach
The homes and hearts behind us.
Should e'er they touch our dear lov'd shores, &c.

Though men of peace, if war should come,
In friendship's lap while lying,
The lamb will then a lion turn,
The Eagle's brood defying,
And shake in wrath his shaggy mane :
Then foremost you shall find us,
The Volunteers, to shield from harm
The homes and hearts behind us.
And shake in wrath his shaggy mane &c.

November.

Infant Winter, young November,
  Nursling of the glowing woods,
Lo! the sleep is burst that bound thee—
Lift thine eyes above, around thee,
  Infant sire of storm and floods.

Through the tangled green and golden
  Curtains of thy valley bed,
See the trees hath vied to woo thee,
And with homage to subdue thee—
  Show'ring bright leaves o'er thy head.

Let, oh! let their fading glories
  Grace the earth while still they may,
For the poplar's-orange, gleaming,
And the beech's ruddy beaming,
  Warmer seems to make the day.

Now the massy plane-leaf's twirling,
  Down the misty morning light,

And the saugh-tree's tinted treasure
Seems to seek the earth with pleasure—
  Show'ring down from morn till night.

Through the seasons, ever varying,
  Rapture fills the human soul;
Blessed dower! to mankind given,
All is perfect under heaven,
  In the part as in the whole.

Hush'd the golden flute of mavis,
  Silver pipe of little wren,
But the readbreast's notes are ringing,
And its "weel-kent" breast is bringing
  Storied boyhood back again.

Woodland splendour of November,
  Did departing Autumn dye
All thy foliage, that when roamin'
We might pictur'd—see her gloamin'
  In thy woods as in her sky.

The Poet's Last Song.

Heart—heart be still,
　Thy fond aspirings cease,
Thy cup of misery soon shall fill—
　So be at peace.

Life! fleeting life!
　Thy sunniest hours are past,
Why seek thee to prolong the dark'ning strife
　With it to last.

Bring me my lyre,
　I yet may sweep its strings,
'Twill aid the visions that life's flickering fire
　In rapture brings.

Earth! sea! and sky!
　I see thy hallowed spots—
My soul, even now, is treading daringly
　Where beauty floats.

Round sunny hill—
  Now in the leafy grove,
Where birds make music that the soul doth fill
  With thoughts of love.

And thou, dread sea!
  My youthful days return,
Pictured in vision, in my soul, I see
  Thee, and do mourn:

That I may ne'er
  Again lie on thy breast,
Pillow my cheek upon thy waves, nor e'er
  Break thy foam crest.

God of the sky—
  How oft at eventide,
When thou to rest were sinking gloriously,
  Have I beside
Some ruin gray,
Knelt down and worshipped thee!

          .   .   .   .

'Tis broke—'tis broke—
  The chain is snapt—the link
Of being sever'd—man living—death may mock
  Not on the brink

Where life meets death.
 My song is done—away!
Open the lattice that the summer's breath
 May coolly play

Upon my brow.
 Life now throbs—fitfully—
By starts 'tis calm, as if it linger'd—now
 On wings I fly
To love and home—
 I see them vividly—

  . . . .

Now let me die.

Copied from "The Day" of April 18th, 1832.

A Sister's Love.

My sister's tones—how sweetly they
 Are mingled in my midnight dreams;
Like silv'ry sounds from golden harps,
 Attun'd to love's delicious themes.

Oh! I have felt a lover's love,
   With all its dear and painful thrilling;
And I have heard a lov'd one's voice,
   When flowery sweets the air were filling,
Breathing the vow with downcast eye,
   Of never-failing constancy.

A mother's voice I've heard arise
In grief fraught-tones, in boding sighs;
While throbbing beat each pulse and vein,
As if they ne'er would beat again.

A father's prayers—they, too, have shed
Their sacred influence round my bed;
While deep and holy rose the lays
Of heartfelt gratitude and praise.

But when sleep, o'er my weary eyes,
   Would hover near with all its bliss,
With stealthy step my sister came—
   Imprinted on my brow her kiss;
Sat by my couch the while I slumber'd,
Nor weary hours of watching number'd—
Breathed her pure love—when none were near—
And dropp'd upon my cheek her tear;

And when I woke, her voice and eye
Were sweet as bow'rs of Araby—
A mother's sigh, a lov'd one's kiss,
A father's prayer seemed nought to this.

On J. W. falling heir to considerable property.

"So Johnny he's an heir!
An' if ye observe it,
Seldom sic gude luck
Fa's where they deserve it."

Sic a hearty cheer
Frae his trusty cronies,
Weel might warm a heart
Caulder far than Johnny's.

When we're growin' auld,
To provide a mouthfu'
Is a weary faught,—
No to say a toothfu'.

Then when Fortune comes
Like a show'r in summer,
Scattering riches roon,
Welcome is the kimmer.

He's got bills an' bonds,
Three per cents, an' real stock,
An' as meikle gowd
As will fill a meal pock.

Will it drive him gyte—
Will he turn deleerit—
Will he aff to France—
Or to some place near it?

Puddocks eat, an' learn
Capering an' booin',
Tyne his mither-tongue,
An' tak to parley-vooin'.

Will he treat his gab
To their ham sae reekie,
Sup oysters wi' a spoon
Yet bock at cockie-leekie?

Will subscription sheets
　　Handsomely be arl'd,
That his name may be
　　Foremost in the "Herald?"

Will he buy a wig
　　Shinin' like a fiddle,
Specs without e'en shanks
　　On his nose to striddle?

Rin an' ring the bell,—
　　Tell each worthy cronie,
Siller mak's nae change
　　For the waur on Johnnie.

Aye the hearty laugh,
　　Aye the langsyne story,
Aye the tither tot,
　　An' Johnnie's in his glory!

Cowe the Nettle Early.

AIR—"Whistle o'er the Lave o't."

Wandering through the woods in spring,
Thus a weel kent voice did sing,
"Wither'd age nae joys can bring,
    I'll cowe the nettle early."

"Wha for walth wad ane that's auld
In their youthfu' arms enfauld ?
O they're gruesome, rough, an' cauld.
    I'll cowe the nettle early."

"When in love we're mim an' meek,
Unco shy an' laith to speak,
But the blush that tints our cheek,
    Says cowe the nettle early."

Thus my lassie to hersel'
Liltin' made my bosom swell ;
Rin an' ring the parish bell,
    We'll cowe the nettle early.

I've been warm'd with ruddy wine—
Dreamt of calling riches mine,
There's a pleasure more divine,
    I'll cowe the nettle early.

On the Marriage of Robert K—n, Esq.

TO HENRY HEANY, ESQ.

Sir,

    On this interesting epoch in the life of Robert K——n, viz:—his union with the amiable and accomplished Miss Glass, he will receive the congratulations of his numerous friends.

    I have presumed to imagine that which you jocularly but sincerely might say—and in a postscript, what I, without any joke at all, and, I am certain, as sincerely, would say.

Yours truly,

WILLIAM MILLER.

Let social friends and all good men
    Rejoice, nor cry alas!
Though K——n, such a sober youth,
    Has vowed to take a *Glass*.

Let no weak fears molest our minds,
    That poverty and strife
Will be his lot, though he has sworn
    To take a Glass through life.

But let us hope with fervency
(Our love for him is such)
That at the close of life he'll say,
I ne'er took *one too much.*

And may he find when troubles come,
And all looks dark and drear,
His Glass more potent then than now
To strengthen and to cheer.

P. S.—But this I hope he won't forget,
Amid his marriage fuss,
Tho' he has got a Glass himself,
To order one for us.

For gentlemen who win a race—
And love a race is found—
Although they take but one themselves,
Do order glasses round.

And so he did, and so we got
All brimful glasses each ;
But such a Glass as he has got
There's none of us can reach.

The sequel is, all of us got
Full glasses every one—
The Glass which he has got we wish
He never will see done.

Ane an' be Dune wi't.

If folk wad be cautious when takin' a drappy,
And mind they maun eat as weel's drink to be happy,
They'd be better acquaint wi' the grocer and dealer,
Nor be shouther-for-shouther wi' beagle or jailor:—
They micht blaw their ain whistle, and play a gude tune wi't,
If they had but the sense to tak' ane an' be dune wi't;
 Ane an' be dune wi't, ane an' be dune wi't—
 An' no to be daidlin' frae Tintock to Troon wi't,
 An' wastin' their time,—but tak' ane an' be dune wi't.

A dram wi' an auld frien', I ne'er saw the harm in't;
In gi'en an' takin', there's something sae warm in't,
Ane sits rather langer than maybe he should do,

An' spends somethin' mair than he otherwise would do—
The night has its pleasures, but morning this croon wi't—
Aye tak' my advice, just tak' ane an' be dune wi't;
    Ane an' be dune wi't, ane an' be dune wi't—
    An' dinna be sochrin' frae July to June wi't,
    An' wastin' your time, but tak' ane an' be dune wi't.

A cheerie gudewife, wi' a smile where a frown was,
That helpit ye up, aye, in a' your bit downfa's;
A cup o' gude tea, then, instead o' your drummock ;
A groat in your pouch, for a gill in your stomach ;
A guid coat on your back, and a pair o' new shoon wi't—
O these are the comforts o' ane an' be dune wi't—
    Ane an' be dune wi't, ane an' be dune wi't;
    For folk wha are tipplin' [a] hale winter's moon wi't
    Are laughed at for fools,—so tak' ane an' be dune wi't.

O Listen to Me, Love.

O listen to me, love, an' mark what I say—
Thinkna my love's like a fause April day,
Kything in sunshine, an' setting in show'r,
Leaving in ruin the noon-cherish'd flow'r.

No, lassie, no: thou hast seen the lark rise,
Warbling and soaring his way to the skies,
Farther frae a' he loves, warmer his lay,
So will my true heart be—mark what I say.

I ken that you lo'e me, by that tear let fa'
On my han' that's a fondlin' thy jimp waist sae sma'
An' young love a-stealing the rose frae thy cheek,
For fear that in blushes the truth it wad speak.

The night gathers round us, I scarcely can see
The ane that is mair than the warld to me,
But her wee han's soft pressure like kind words did say,
I'm yours, Willie only, yours only, for aye.

I Had a Dream.

I had o' ither days,
  A sinless dream o' joy;
It came like sunshine o'er a clud,
  Life's dark spots to destroy.

It came when I was sick at heart,
  And sleepless was mine e'e,
When luve was fause, and wily tongue
  Turn'd frien' to enemie.

I thought a saft han' lay in mine,
  A sma' waist in my arm,
A wee heart beating, throbbing fast,
  Wi' luve an' life bluid-warm.

A dreamy spell lay on our lips,
  A luve-band round our hearts;
But, as by magic, her blue e'en
  Tauld ilk thocht that did start.

In quiet streams I've seen fair flow'rs,
　Hid 'neath the bank they grew;
Sae in her deep blue e'en I read
　Flow'r-thochts o' various hue.

"O dinna luik sae kind, Willie,
　Or else wi' joy I'll dee,
An' dinna read my heart, Willie,
　Wi' thae lang luiks o' your eye.

A maiden's heart should be, Willie,
　A sacred thing to men;
Its workin's in an hour o' joy
　Man-body ne'er can ken.

The flow'r that in the shade wad leeve,
　Will wither in the sun—
An' joy may work on maiden heart
　What grief wad ne'er ha'e dune."

The marrin' o' a melody,
　The stoppin' o' a stream,
A sudden lapse in sunny licht,
　The burstin' o' a dream!

I woke—and on my glassy e'en
 The paley morn-beams shone,—
"Speak on," I cried, "speak on," but lo!
 The weel-kent voice was gone.

Tell her Mither.

When the wind is in the north,
 Keep the house, says her mither;
When the wind is in the north,
 Keep the house;
For the winds are over bauld,
And ye're sure to catch the cauld—
Ye'll be croighlin twa-fauld,
 Says her mither, says her mither—
 Ye'll be croighlin twa-fauld, says her mither.

When the wind is in the east,
 Keep the house, says her mither;
When the wind is in the east,
 Keep the house—

Gaun stravagin' in the dark,
By the dykeside or the park,
Is nae silly body's wark,
  Says her mither, says her mither,
    Is nae silly body's wark, says her mither.

But the lassie's heart's my ain,
  Tell her mither, tell her mither;
But the lassie's heart's my ain,
  Tell her mither;
And ae fauld o' Willie's arm,
Tho' it had nae ither charm,
Can keep a' within it warm—
  Tell her mither, tell her mither,
    Can keep a' within it warm, tell her mither.

To a Bat.

Methinks 'tis strange to see thee in the city,
　Fluttering above the busy haunts of men
As if bewilder'd with its ceaseless noise,
　Seeking thy ruin'd tow'rs and woods again;

Where shadowy oaks their giant arms are flinging,
　Guarding some remnant of departed glory;
Where wall-flower, fern, and lichen-gray are singing,
　Breeze-touched, to the pale moon, a dirge-like story.

Thou labour'st in thy flight, as if thy spirit,
　Sick with its wanderings, sought a resting spot—
Ah! who may tell the feverish fears that stir it,
　Panting, desponding, for its native grot.

Thou hast forsook the loaning, cool and quiet,
　Soft whispering aspen, dewy beechen tree,
Old castle tower and myrtle haunt, for riot
　That lifts its voice in loud, unhallow'd glee.

Thus, voiceless wanderer, may thy untold woe
   Teach me aright this lesson in my youth—
If passion leads me virtue to forego,
   Yearning again to seek the paths of truth.

The Peasant Bard.

A peasant bard, with song went forth
   To woo the maid he loved;
He sung, and won the maid,—but lo!
   All other hearts he moved.

His warm appeal did fondly steal
   Through bosoms far and near,
And distant hearts confessed the art
   Of him, their minstrel dear.

The planets, in their wondrous course,
   Shall bear his fame along;
The "lingering star" still drops a tear
   To grief's seraphic song.

The "unclouded moon" that shines aboon,
    In pure refulgent light,
From pole to pole shall stir the soul
    On every Lammas night.

The peasant's brow no more shall low'r
    Beneath a lordling's scorn—
Their hearts enshrine the noble thoughts
    Of him, the cottage-born.

Ilk Ane Kens their ain Ken.

Ilk ane kens their ain ken,
    Tho' sair to thole an' hide it O,
But blessin's on our auld Scotch pride,
    There's nane daur e'er deride it, O.
        · Ilk ane kens, &c.

There's mony bear the frowns o' life
    As blythe as love new married, O,

An' hides't in a proud heart's nook,
 As if 'twere smiles they carried, O.
   Ilk ane kens, &c.

He that on fortune's toorie sits
 May fa' an' fin' the hap o't, O,
An' him that's bendin' to the brae
 May ride yet on the tap o't, O.
   Ilk ane kens, &c.

Gi'e me the warm an' furthy heart,
 A han' that ne'er was steekit, O,
To lift the woe frae that strong breast
 That wad rather brust than speak it, O.
   Ilk ane kens, &c.

To the New-Year.

O, come awa', thou hopefu' year!
 A welcome sicht are ye ;
Ye're punctual to a minute, but
 I've weari't sair for thee,—

Ye'll ken I had a craw to pook
   Wi' *her* that's gane, yet nae
Back-spangs at parting e'er should mar
   The mirth o' Hogmanay.

I mind when first she stepped owre
   The threshold o' my door,
That joy led ben the blythesome queen,
   And hope stept on before;
And thick-an'-threefauld in the trance,
   Bright forms strain'd to be near,
The glowing hearth, where hope and joy
   Stood wi' the New-year.

The scourin'-things aboon the brace
   Were bright as han's could mak',
And mony an hour stown frae her sleep,
   My wifie they did tak';
The fire, the floor, the whiten'd wa's,
   The bowls upon the dresser,
Blythe faces, too, and happy hearts
   Had welcomes warm to bless her.

My callant then had gat new claes,
   So ripe his gather'd glee,
That joy bow'd doon to kiss his lip,
   His lip an' loupin' e'e;

Atween the breenges o' his mouth,
  .Hope tauld him many a story,
An' pointed forth to simmer days
  And a' their gowan glory.

Aye, youth! loup up an kiss the mou'
  O' rosy lipped joy!
Believe in hope's most wondrous tales
  Whilst thou art yet a boy—
Thy present always be as now,
  A merry Hogmanay;
Thy future in ilk comin' morn
  A Happy New-year's-day!

To Jessica.

The noon's fleecy brightness, the evening's gray calm,
May pour o'er my spirit their gladness or balm;
The hoary oak bend 'neath the blast of the north,
When like a stern giant the storm rideth forth—

But thy beauty is brighter than noon in its power,
Thy mildness more balmy than evening's calm hour,
And thy voice o'er my spirit sweeps stronger by far
Than the blast fiercely rushing from tempest's dark car.

When the flowers of the earth into odours arise,
And their guardian sprites bear their bloom to the skies,
Then rainbow is bound like a garland round earth,
As maidens do garnish loved ones in their mirth;
But when from thy lips I a love-token seek
The love of thy heart blushes red on thy cheek—
Then a rainbow-like halo is bound round my heart,
A garland of gladness, that ne'er can depart.

Ye Cowe a'.

AIR.—"Comin' through the Rye."

I wiled my lass wi' loving words to Kelvin's leafy shade,
And a' that fondest heart can feel, or tongue can tell I said;

But nae reply my lassie gied—I blam'd the waterfa',
Its deavin' soun' my voice did drown—O this cowes a'!
 O this cowes a', quo I, O this cowes a'!
 I wonder how the birds can woo—O this cowes a'!

I wiled my lass wi' loving words to Kelvin's solemn grove,
Where silence, in her dewy bowers, hush'd a' sounds but o' love;
Still frae my earnest looks and vows, she turned her head awa',
Nae cheering word the silence heard—O this cowes a'!
 O this cowes a', quo' I, O this cowes a'!
 To woo I'll try anither way, for this cowes a'!

I wiled my lass wi' loving words to where the moonlight fell,
Upon a bank of blooming flowers, beside the pear-tree well;
Say, modest moon, did I do wrang to clasp her waist sae sma'
And steal ae kiss o' honied bliss?—O, ye cowe a'!
 O ye cowe a', quo' she, O ye cowe a'!
 Ye might ha'e speer'd a body's leave—but ye cowe a'!

I'll to the clerk, quo' I, sweet lass, on Sunday we'll be cried,
And frae your father's house, next day, ye'll gang a dear lo'ed bride—
Quo' she, I'd need anither week to mak' a gown mair braw—
The gown ye ha'e we'll mak it do—O ye cowe a'!
 O ye cowe a', quo' she, O ye cowe a',
 But wilfu' folk maun ha'e their way—O ye cowe a'!

Hogmanay.

This is the last night o' this year, lads,
    Let come in the next whate'er may ;
He that's eydent and honest can welcome
    The morning o' ilk New-year's-day.

'Tis only the knave needs be gloomy,
    When thinking on what he has done ;
But we blythely will sing in the morning,
    And dance by the light o' the moon.

There's muckle in this world to grieve us—
    I doutna we've a' had our share—
But to warsle an' win is a pleasure,
    And what can a mortal do mair ?

The mile-stanes o' life, as we journey,
    Are lang weary twalmonths atween ;
Let us rest an' look back, an' mak' merry,
    When we meet wi' an honest auld frien'.

Then, Johnnie,* come fill us a jorum,
  And Gib he will sing us a sang,
That will keep frien'ship warm in our bosoms
  To anither mile-stane, as we gang.

Be Kind to Grandfather.

Be kind to grandfather,—a proud man was he
When rosy in childhood ye sat on his knee;
Thy name is his name, when his head is laid low,
May his virtues be link'd wi' the name o' his oe.

He led thy young feet where the buttercups grew
An' gowans were thickest, an' pu'd them for you;
But wad glint, lest the neebors or ony might see,
And say that the auld fule was ower proud o' thee.

By Parkhead's nameless burnie, where rashes did grow,
A cap he wad weave for thy fair curly pow,
An' a boat wi' a string,—when you led it alane
In your glee, the auld man was a bairn ance again.

*Mr. John Watson and Mr. Gilbert Watson, Parkhead.

I ha'e seen the big tear, when he thocht nae ane saw,
Heard the lang thochtfu' sigh, that the auld heart can draw,
An' I'm sure that he prayed, and its burthen wad be
That the e'e o' the Watchfu' wad watch over thee.

When tott'rin wi' age, now, an' bent owre a rung,
The peace he inherits he wrought for when young;
An' when ye were a wean, as he chirm'd ye asleep,
He wad sing—Willie, mind, as ye sow ye will reap.

Lightburn Glen.

AIR—" There was a Lass, and she was fair."

There is a spot I dearly lo'ed,
    When I was summers nine or ten,
Where slender blue-bells wav'd and woo'd
    Young barefoot wanderers to that glen.
So shy the wagtail bobb'd and bow'd—
    A mystery was the little wren—
And purple berries there were pu'd
    By laughin' bands in Lightburn Glen.

When gloamin breath'd upon thy stream,
    And hush'd the song of roaming bee,
Ere yet the moon had lent her beam
    To make thee lovelier, if might be;
Then still the lark proclaimed thy praise,
    And challeng'd in his song divine
Those glorious two,* whose mellow lays
    Charm'd the dark woods of Carntyne.

Another beauty met my gaze
    In riper years, with all to join—
That lark might ne'er attempt to praise,
    Nor all the choir of Carntyne.
If ye ha'e woo'd and hae'na won,
    By dewy loan or leafy den;
There's no a place below the sun
    I'd sooner try than Lightburn Glen.

*Those glorious two—the blackbird and mavis.

To my Coat.

Though hardly worth one paltry groat,
Thou'rt dear to me, my poor old coat,
For full ten years my friend thou'st been,
For full ten years I've brush'd thee clean;
And now, like me, thou'rt old and wan,
With both the glow of youth is gone—
But, worn and shabby as thou art,
Thou and the poet shall not part.

Poor coat.

I've not forgot the birth-day eve,
When first I donned thy glossy sleeve,
When jovial *friends*, in mantling wine,
Drank joy and health to me and mine.
Our indigence let some despise,
We're dear as ever in *their* eyes
And for their sakes, old as thou art,
Thou and the poet shall not part,

Poor coat.

One evening, I remember yet,
I, romping, feigned to fly Lisette—
She strove her lover to retain,
And thy frail skirt was rent in twain,—
Dear girl, she did her best endeavour,
And patched thee up as well as ever;
For her sweet sake, old as thou art,
Thou and the poet shall not part,
                              Poor coat.

Never, my coat, hast thou been found
Bending thy shoulders to the ground,
From any upstart, "Lord" or "Grace,"
To beg a pension or a place
Wild forest flowers—no monarch's dole
Adorn thy modest button-hole;
If, but for that, old as thou art,
Thou and the poet shall not part,
                              Poor coat.

Poor though we be, my good old friend,
No gold shall bribe our backs to bend;
Honest amid temptations past,
We will be honest to the last—

For more I prize thy virtuous rags
Than all the lace a courtier brags,
And while I live, and have a heart,
Thou and the poet shall not part,

My coat.

—Translated from Beranger.

A Pretty Idea.

Cupid, near a cradle creeping,
Saw an infant gently sleeping,
The rose that blush'd upon its cheek
Seem'd a birth divine to speak:
To ascertain if earth or heaven
To mortals this fair form had given,
He, the little urchin simple,
Touched its cheek, and left a *dimple*.

—From a Staffordshire Newspaper.

To Peter M'D——.

RESPECTFULLY INSCRIBED TO PETER M'DONALD, ESQ.

"Aye follow your calling wi' steady endeavour,
In firmness o' purpose, that naething can waver;
And you'll find in your youth, that your fortune is mending,
If you manage to mak' daily mair than you're spending;
And, believe me, the auld proverb's true to the letter—
'The less that you need, your friends like you the better,'
'And, the publican's fireside's the dearest, you'll see,"
Siclike were the sayings o' Peter M'D——.

O the worth o' that parent, whose precepts he treasured,
And the love o' that mither's heart!—ne'er to be measnred—
Wha morning and e'en, saft as simmer's wind moanest,
Sang, " Bairnie, hae pride, though you're poor aye be honest,
Keep back frae the cheatrei, nor do to anither
What wad bring a tear to the e'e o' your mither—
That the red flash o' shame on her cheek ne'er may be,
By the sayings or doings o' Peter M'D——."

So he grew up a man, wi' a fortified heart
'Gainst a' kinds o' roguery, in airt or in pairt;
Though he's often been trick'd by the smooth-lipped knave,
And wrong'd by the ane he assisted to save—
He ne'er stoop'd to the meanness o' fraud and deceit,
To mak' up his losses, although they were great;
And Providence pour'd, like a spate o'er the lea,
Baith business and wealth upon Peter M'D——.

As a master, though gleg—yet o'erlooking a faut
In the shape o' a dram, nor lets on that he saw't;
And the ne'er-do-weel loon, be it said to his shame,
When there's nought but the bare wa's to look on at hame,
Comes to him wi' his plaint, a sma' pittance to spare
To keep wife an' weans frae the sheugh o' despair—
Like the bite an' the buffet a mither does gi'e,
Came the crown an' the counsel, frae Peter M'D——.

Though no a bred scholar, his judgment is such,
He staps to conclusions ere logic can touch;
At a twa-handed crack o'er some kittle laid plan,
Ye'll find ye ha'e met wi' a sensible man;
Wha the fop'ries o' speech can afford to disdain,
And in guid hamely Scotch, a' he thinks can explain;
Nae chains round his neck, nor glass stuck on his e'e,
Nor rings on his fingers, need Peter M'D——.

Lang may you be spared! now the haffets are gray
I've seen black as the raven, in life's early day;
Though hearty thy laugh, and thy joke cheerfu' still
The e'enin' will come, the sun sink o'er the hill.
While the sands o' thy days are permitted to run,
May you hear your gear spoke o' as gear honest won;
At lang an'-the-last then, when life tak's the gee,
May we shake han's, to meet again, Peter M'D——.

www.ingramcontent.com/pod-product-compliance
Lightning Source LLC
Chambersburg PA
CBHW020251090426
42735CB00010B/1883